Philippians

DISCOVER TOGETHER BIBLE STUDY SERIES

Leader's guides are available at www.discovertogetherseries.com

A *Discover Together* BIBLE STUDY

Philippians

Discovering Joy Through Relationship

Sue Edwards

Kregel
Publications

Published by Kregel Publications, a division of Kregel, Inc., 2450 Oak Industrial Dr. NE, Grand Rapids, MI 49505

ISBN 978-0-8254-4399-2

Contents

How to Get the Most Out of a Discover Together Bible Study

Women today need Bible study to keep balanced, focused, and Christ-centered in their busy worlds. The tiered questions in *Philippians: Discovering Joy Through Relationship* allow you to choose a depth of study that fits your lifestyle, which may even vary from week to week, depending on your schedule.

Just completing the basic questions will require about one and a half hours per lesson, and will provide a basic overview of the text. For busy women, this level offers in-depth Bible study with a minimum time commitment.

"Digging Deeper" questions are for those who want to, and make time to, probe the text even more deeply. Answering these questions may require outside resources such as an atlas, Bible dictionary, or concordance; you may be asked to look up parallel passages for additional insight; or you may be encouraged to investigate the passage using an interlinear Greek-English text or *Vine's Expository Dictionary*. This deeper study will challenge you to learn more about the history, culture, and geography related to the Bible, and to grapple with complex theological issues and differing views. Some with teaching gifts and an interest in advanced academics will enjoy exploring the depths of a passage, and might even find themselves creating outlines and charts and writing essays worthy of seminarians!

This inductive Bible study is designed for both individual and group discovery. You will benefit most if you tackle each week's lesson on your own, and then meet with other women to share insights, struggles, and aha moments. Bible study leaders will find free, downloadable leader's guides for each study, along with general tips for leading small groups, at www.discovertogetherseries.com.

Through short video clips, Sue Edwards shares personal insights to enrich your Bible study experience. You can watch these as you work through each lesson on your own, or your Bible study leader may want your whole study group to view them when you meet together. For ease of individual viewing, a QR code, which you can simply scan with your smartphone, is

provided in each lesson. Or you can go to www.discovertogetherseries.com and easily navigate until you find the corresponding video title. Woman-to-woman, these clips are meant to bless, encourage, and challenge you in your daily walk.

Choose a realistic level of Bible study that fits your schedule. You may want to finish the basic questions first, and then "dig deeper" as time permits. Take time to savor the questions, and don't rush through the application. Watch the videos. Read the sidebars for additional insight to enrich the experience. Note the optional passage to memorize and determine if this discipline would be helpful for you. Do not allow yourself to be intimidated by women who have more time or who are gifted differently.

Make your Bible study—whatever level you choose—top priority. Consider spacing your study throughout the week so that you can take time to ponder and meditate on what the Holy Spirit is teaching you. Do not make other appointments during the group Bible study. Ask God to enable you to attend faithfully. Come with an excitement to learn from others and a desire to share yourself and your journey. Give it your best, and God promises to join you on this adventure that can change your life.

Why Study Philippians?

Most studies on the Philippian letter emphasize Paul's remarkable joy springing from almost every verse, remarkable because he penned the letter while confined under house arrest in Rome. Certainly a noteworthy observation, especially in light of Paul's adventurous life. Now this type A energizer was forced to carry on his missionary work chained to a Roman guard. But as I devoured the letter in my personal study, I also saw two powerful resources enabling Paul to bear fruit in chains: first, of course, was his robust relationship with God; but second, and less often considered, was his staunch friendships with the Philippians. In our study, we'll focus on both Paul's ability to rise above his circumstances *and* the part friends played in his success.

Paul was relational, and in Philippians he models the beauty and power of authentic Christian community, something most of us crave, especially in our networked lives. Today, many of us are more connected superficially through technology, but less connected in "keep it real," face-to-face relationships. The Bible assumes, however, that Christians will support one another through good times and bad. The Philippian letter illustrates this assumption. We were all made for community and we cannot thrive without it.

The letter is jam-packed with plural pronouns and statements like, "I thank my God every time I remember you. In all my prayers for all of you, I always pray with joy because of your partnership in the gospel from the first day until now. . . . It is right for me to feel this way about all of you, since I have you in my heart and, whether I am in chains or defending and confirming the gospel, all of you share in God's grace with me. God can testify how I long for all of you with the affection of Christ Jesus" (Philippians 1:3–5, 7–8). Paul knew how to encourage and exhort his friends, and God wants us to learn how too. Studying this little letter will show us ways to love our friends well.

These tender connections began on Paul's second missionary journey when God called him to plant the first church on the European continent. The place was Philippi, a Roman colony and leading city in the region.

In lesson 1, we'll meet the unique characters who became some of Paul's dearest friends.

As you work through the lessons, look for this constant communal theme and Paul's resulting joy, even in tough times. Being anchored in healthy community will also help us through tough times. How would your life be different if you lived in Philippi where tight-knit, supportive community was the norm? What are you missing out on today because you are failing to invest in the life of the church? How might you create a place where you don't think in terms of "me" but in terms of "we"? Welcome to the little letter that just might make a big difference in your life.

 Introduction to Studying Philippians *(11:06 minutes).*

Beloved Friendships | LESSON 1

I love people, but that hasn't always been true. If people hurt us, we often struggle to trust them. That's what happened to me. But when I was in my mid-twenties, a neighbor invited me to a women's Bible study where a team of godly Christian women introduced me to Jesus. They also loved me and taught me what true friendships look like. Those relationships changed my life. And ever since, God has blessed me with dear friends who point me to the Lord and make me better than I could ever be without their prayers, encouragement, and guidance. The letter we are about to study was written by a man who loved and valued his friends too. Paul was relational.

I've heard several pastors define what's really important in life this way: only two things on earth will last for eternity, the truth of God's word and people. I think Paul would agree. Most of us desire enriching relationships in which we can be real and give others the same freedom. Do you want to experience those kinds of relationships? Watch Paul and the Philippians. As we dig into the Philippian letter, we will observe beautiful friendships, up close and personal. Those relationships model how intimate, authentic friends treat one another, even when relationships turn messy and complicated.

OPTIONAL

Memorize Philippians 1:3–6

I thank my God every time I remember you. In all my prayers for all of you, I always pray with joy because of your partnership in the gospel from the first day until now, being confident of this, that he who began a good work in you will carry it on to completion until the day of Christ Jesus.

 Joy Through Relationship (*13:00 minutes*).

But before we dig into the letter, I want you to see how God sovereignly connected Paul with his friends in Philippi. These people worked with Paul to birth the church there. How did God supernaturally bring them together? What kinds of people were they? How did Paul woo and win them to Jesus? What experiences gave them a common history that made their lives together richer, more productive, and sweet? Our story begins in Acts 16:6–40.

Read Acts 16:6–10.

Paul, Silas, and Timothy are revisiting churches that Paul planted on his first mission trip. His desire was to encourage them and to see how they were progressing. Many of thechurches Paul planted on his first missionary journey were in Asia Minor, now Turkey.

1. Their plan was to visit churches in that region, but why did they abandon their original itinerary (16:6–7)?

A tragic thing happens to us when we outplan God and resist his interventions because they were not on our carefully calculated agendas.
  —Lloyd John Ogilve (*Drumbeat of Love*, 201)

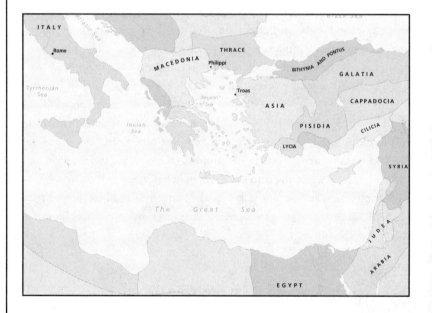

2. Name some ways God redirects people today. Can you think of specific examples? (No names, please.)

See, I am doing a new thing! Now it springs up; do you not perceive it? I am making a way in the wilderness and streams in the wasteland.
  —Isaiah 43:19

DIGGING DEEPER

Who has joined Paul's group? How do you know (16:10)?

3. Has "the Holy Spirit" or "the Spirit of Jesus" ever rerouted your own journey? How did you know it was God guiding you in a different direction?

4. Where did Paul go instead (16:8)? Who sought his help? How (16:9)? What was Paul's response (16:10)?

5. To guide Paul into Europe (Macedonia), God had to close a door to the south and to the north. Has God ever closed doors for you? If so, when? How did you feel? What did God have planned instead?

Read Acts 16:11–15.

On to Philippi, a Roman colony and leading city of Macedonia on the continent of Europe. Philippi was named after Philip of Macedon, Alexander the Great's father.

6. Paul's practice was to search out a synagogue and explain the gospel there first. Since apparently there was no synagogue in Philippi, where did Paul go to begin his ministry? Who was there? Describe the first convert in Europe. (16:13–14)

DIGGING DEEPER

Why might one argue that the Trinity was involved in guiding these missionaries to the continent of Europe?

Authentic turning points in history are few. But surely among them that of the Macedonian vision ranks high. Because of Paul's obedience at this point, the gospel went westward; and ultimately Europe and the Western world were evangelized. Christian response to the call of God is never a trivial thing. Indeed, as in this instance, great issues and untold blessings may depend on it.
—Richard N. Longenecker
("Acts," 458)

This passage has become popular because in it God gave Paul definite guidance concerning where He wanted him to minister. Anyone who wants to propagate the gospel has questions about this kind of guidance. Notice that Paul was actively ministering and was seeking to do what appeared to him to be the wise thing when God said no and yes to his efforts. In providing positive direction, God brought new information to Paul that impressed the apostle with a particular need that God wanted him to meet. It seems to me that we should not concern ourselves mainly with the methods God uses to guide people. These varied in Acts and were not Luke's primary concern. We should, however, concentrate on where we can be of most use as the Lord's servants. This was Paul's dominant concern. If our choices for places of ministry are equally acceptable to God, He probably will not steer us away from any of them, as was true in Paul's first missionary journey. We can go wherever we please. However, if He does not want us in one or more of these places, I believe He will shut one or more doors for us as He did for Paul. God often guides us by bringing information to our attention that enlightens our judgment when we need to make decisions.
—Thomas L. Constable
(Notes on Acts, 233)

7. How did the first convert in Europe express faith (16:15)?

If you travel to the ancient ruins of Philippi, you can stand on a bridge that overlooks a stream outside the ancient city gate where many believe Paul and his fellow travelers first met Lydia and the other women "God worshippers." When I was there, I sensed God's presence in a special way. I remember peering into the bubbling crystal clear stream as it rushed by us while our seminary president read of the account. We took communion there to celebrate what Jesus did to bring salvation to the Gentiles as well as the Jews. I can't wait to meet Lydia, the first convert from Europe. Paul is often characterized as a woman-hater, but if he was, he would not have ministered to these women beside the river. But he did. He ministered to them by the river during a time in history when women were seen as inferior and personal contact with them was sometimes suspect. We have no evidence that other men from the city were present. Jesus's care and concern for women must have rubbed off on this former Pharisee, and as a result, Paul introduced the women to Jesus. As a result, Lydia became an influential and founding member of the Philippian church. What an encouragement to Christian women everywhere! —Sue

Because no husband is mentioned, we can speculate that Lydia was a widow. We can also surmise that as a dealer in purple cloth, she was probably quite wealthy. During the Roman era, only the rich and privileged were allowed to wear the color purple. Purple dye was collected drop by drop from a certain shellfish. Lydia's business catered to well-to-do customers. And her home was large enough to accommodate Paul and the others in their party while they were in Philippi, and may have been the meeting place for the infant church after Paul left. Women in the first century often used their influence and wealth to serve as patronesses, and it's likely that Lydia used her influence to help the new church "find its feet."

Read Acts 16:16–40.

8. Who made ministry in Philippi difficult for Paul? How? (16:16–17)

9. According to verse 18, what did she do that caused Paul to stop ignoring her? How did Paul respond?

10. How did the owners react when they realized their business enterprise was ruined (16:19–21)?

11. Specifically, what did Paul and Silas endure in 16:22–24? Imagine this happened to you. How would you feel? How do you normally react when you are treated unfairly or suffer unjustly? How do you think you might react if you found yourself in Paul's and Silas's stocks?

12. How did Paul and Silas respond (16:25)? How did their response affect the other prisoners (see 16:28)?

13. How did God supernaturally rescue them? What happened to the prison and the other prisoners as a result? (16:26) How might typical prisoners respond if this occurred?

14. What was the jailer going to do as a result? Why? (16:27)

15. How did Paul stop him (16:28)? Why do you think the prisoners had not tried to escape?

16. The jailer then fell trembling before Paul and Silas (16:29). In your opinion, why (16:30)? Why do you think the jailer knew that he needed to be "saved"?

Today, sex traffickers enslave adolescents and adults, using and abusing them to earn money for themselves. These abominable practices occur all over the world, including within the United States. To learn about some ministries that work to end trafficking and exploitation as well as minister to victims and raise awareness, see www.love146 .org, www.newfriendsnewlife .org, or www.freethecaptives houston.com.

Author Anneke Companjen travels with her missionary husband, the president of Open Doors International, witnessing firsthand the persecution that women endure today in many parts of the world. She introduces her readers to women who learned to "sing through the night" despite their struggles and pain. Read her stories of eleven women from nine different countries who suffered for Christ yet continued to praise and serve the Lord in *Singing Through the Night*.

Roman law required that a jailer suffer his prisoner's punishment if that prisoner escaped.

In 16:15 and 33, we learn that in addition to Lydia and the jailer, their households were baptized, reflecting conversion. In our Western individualistic way of thinking, we may be surprised that whole households would come to faith together. It helps to understand the Eastern mentality of community where families typically made these kinds of decisions together.

17. If someone asked you to answer the jailer's question—"What must I do to be saved?"—what would you say?

18. Who was converted that night? How did they express their newfound faith? (16:31–34)

19. Consider the ways God used Paul to win converts to his church in Philippi. How do you think Paul felt as he looked back over his first few days in Philippi?

20. Share an experience, if you can, when God's ways were unexpected in your life.

21. How did the jailer's treatment of his prisoners change after his conversion (16:24–33)? Do you know anyone who changed dramatically after coming to faith? Share their story if appropriate.

22. In the morning, the jailer probably brought Paul and Silas back to the prison. When the magistrates ordered their release, why do you think Paul insisted upon an apology (16:37–39)? How might this have affected the status of the church that Paul would soon leave behind?

23. Instead of leaving town as the officials requested, where did Paul and Silas go first (16:40)? In your opinion, what was their purpose in staying?

24. Look back over 16:16–40. Which of the people described in these verses *definitely* became Christians? Which do you think *probably* accepted Paul's message of love and redemption and joined the new church Paul founded before he left?

25. How were these new converts different? Compare their backgrounds, experiences, and the way God worked in their lives. What is the lesson for us?

26. Consider some of the challenges these different converts probably experienced as they attempted to worship and work together in the First Church of Philippi. What enables Christians from varied backgrounds and perspectives to thrive as the Body of Christ?

27. About ten years after the experiences recorded in Acts 16, Paul wrote the letter to the Philippians that is recorded in our Bibles. He wrote the letter as a prisoner in a Roman jail. Typically, letters would be read aloud to the entire congregation. Keep in mind the people and circumstances you studied in Acts 16. What do you think might have run through the Philippians' minds as they heard that Paul was in prison again?

28. As we will see when we study the Philippian letter, Paul and the Philippians shared an intimate bond of friendship. Consider how these relationships began. What do you learn about friendships that might help you thrive in relationships that God brings into your life?

An Endearing Prayer | LESSON 2

Nothing we can do, think, or say is more powerful than prayer. Prayer unleashes the armies of heaven. Prayer enables us to see as God sees. Prayer blesses others far more than anything we can do for them. Yet many of us spend more time trying to manipulate people and situations than we do praying. I get this. Prayer can feel inactive and unproductive—until we understand its beauty and power.

For the first ten years of my Christian life, I gave lip service to prayer. I knew prayer was important. I tried to pray faithfully, but I wasn't willing to wait on God or put myself in his hands. I wanted results right now. As I've grown in my walk with Jesus and experienced more of life, I pray more and fret less. I realize that I'm not in control, and neither are you. Prayer is my lifeline to the God who alone is sovereign. He is active in our lives. Praying keeps me centered on him and connected to him, bringing peace and joy.

Praying alone is one thing, but praying out loud with others is another. For me, corporate prayer did not come easily or quickly. But I kept at it. I stopped trying to impress people and I just talked to God, simply and directly. Now I love praying with others. It's a bonding experience and a gift we give our friends.

Paul opens his letter with a heartfelt prayer, a model for us to follow, and a window into his relationships in Philippi. He's writing from Rome. After his missionary journeys, he was arrested and ultimately transported to Rome to await trial. The year is around AD 60 and Paul is under house arrest (Acts 28:16). Nevertheless, his letter reflects a joyful spirit, even though at any moment he could hear the footsteps of executioners who will escort him to the stump and ax. His letter shows us that it is possible to live joyfully in Christ even in the midst of calamity and suffering. And it begins with a beautiful prayer.

Read Philippians 1:1–11.

Ten years have passed since Paul founded the church in Philippi. During these ten years, the Philippian church has grown into a vibrant, mature congregation.

1. How does Paul describe himself to the Philippian congregation? What does he call them? (1:1)

2. Quickly review Lesson 1. As Paul thought about his letter's recipients, who are some of the people he likely had in mind as he wrote?

3. As Paul writes this letter, Roman guards are confining him to a small apartment. How do you think this situation might have affected Paul's daily life? His attitude? Have you ever been shut in your house over a period of time? If so, how did you feel? What do you know about Paul that might have made this confinement particularly difficult?

In verses 3 through 11, Paul reveals his heart for the Philippian believers.

4. How does Paul feel every time he remembers and prays for them (1:3–4)? Why? What do they share? (1:5, 7)

5. How do you think the leaders of your spiritual community feel about you? What do you think comes to mind when they pray for you?

6. Paul uses the term *gospel* more often in this letter than in any of his others. What is the gospel? What do you think he means by this term?

7. Paul says he prays "with joy because of [their] partnership in the gospel from the first day until now" (1:4). In what tangible way had they shared with Paul (see Philippians 4:15–16; 2 Corinthians 8:1–5; 11:9)? What do you learn about the Philippian Christians? What does this tell us about their devotion to him?

8. Have you ever financially supported someone in ministry? If so, describe the situation, how you felt, and how your support benefited the relationship. (No names, please.)

9. From your own life, does anyone specific come to mind when you read Paul's words, "I thank my God every time I remember you" (1:3)? If so, why are you grateful for them? How can gratitude for relationships enrich our lives? Make a plan to express your gratitude to them this week.

10. Who began this "good work" in the lives of the Philippian believers and in their ministry as a church? Who is responsible for carrying it to completion? What do you think Paul means in verse 6? (Note: The "Day of Christ" probably refers to the second coming of Christ.)

11. Has God begun a good work in you? If so, what changes have you observed? What changes would you like to see? Can you hinder God's work in you? If so, how? What are some ways you can cooperate with him as he works in you?

12. What kind of love and affection does Paul feel for the Philippians according to verse 8? See also John 15:9–12; Galatians 5:22; and 1 Corinthians 13:4–6. What are some characteristics of this kind of friendship?

13. As you think of friends you "hold in your heart," what is the basis of your friendship? What can you do to enrich the friendships God has given you or to extend the hand of friendship to others?

Now Paul reveals the content of his prayers for his Philippian friends (1:9–11).

14. What is the key request Paul makes on their behalf (1:9)? In what sense do love and knowledge complement one another?

15. What will result as believers grow in love and knowledge (1:10–11)?

16. What does it mean to be able "to discern what is best" (1:10)? Are you discerning? Can you make choices between what is good and what is best for your life? Share a time when you were required to do so.

17. There are no perfect people (1 John 1:8). In what sense can believers be "pure and blameless" (Philippians 1:10) and "filled with the fruit of righteousness" (1:11) in our lives (see Colossians 2:6–7; 1 John 1:9)?

18. Analyze the content of Paul's prayer in 1:3–11. What elements does it include?

I am overwhelmed by the immensity of the mystery of prayer and the sacred privilege of it. Prayer cannot be summed up in a few pages in a book. It cannot be fully explained or broken down into digestible pieces. . . . I resist any sermon, any teaching that tries to give me a formula for successful prayer. Is an infant's cry diagrammed for success? Doesn't a mother's milk let down at the mere sound of her child's cry? The child of God prays and the Father's compassion gushes forth.
—Jan Winebrenner (*Intimate Faith*, 139)

DIGGING DEEPER

Why do you think Paul speaks of "love" as the source of knowledge instead of the other way around?

The Lord doesn't speak in a whisper or in a dark corner somewhere people can barely hear; nor does He try to trick us because He knows we can't understand what He is saying. "You are my witnesses," declares the Lord, "and my servant whom I have chosen, so that you may know and believe me and understand that I am he" (Isaiah 43:10). God doesn't have a case of cosmic laryngitis and nothing is wrong with His transmitter. Our receiving equipment, however, often leaves a lot to be desired.
—Priscilla Evans Shirer (*He Speaks to Me*, 14)

To be *filled with the fruit of righteousness* for Paul means to go the way of the cross, self-emptying so as to become servant of all in place of "selfish ambition" and, in that servanthood, humbling oneself to the point of dying for another in place of "vain conceit" (2:3–8). . . . This is the righteousness that comes *through Jesus Christ*. All other righteousness, especially religious righteousness, is filth in comparison (3:8).
—Gordon Fee (*Philippians*, 55)

19. Analyze the content of your prayers. Do they contain any of the elements of Paul's prayers for the Philippians?

 Four Tips to Overcome Fear About Praying with Others (*11:27 minutes*).

20. What hinders you from experiencing a rich prayer life? If you are studying *Philippians* with a group of women, how can you help each other overcome these obstacles? If you are studying *Philippians* by yourself, who could help you overcome these obstacles? Make a plan to connect with them this week.

21. How comfortable are you praying out loud for others? What are some of the benefits?

22. How much do you value intercessory prayer for others, and what has it meant in your life?

23. Summarize what you have learned from the first eleven verses of Paul's letter to the Philippians. What is the Holy Spirit asking you to apply to your life this week?

DIGGING DEEPER

Paul's prayer for the Philippians is an example of a biblical prayer that provides a model that teaches us significant lessons on prayer. However, other biblical prayers are instructive too. Spend some time dissecting these passages to learn more about biblical prayer: Abraham's prayer in Genesis 18:16–33; David's prayer in Psalm 51; Hannah's prayer in 1 Samuel 1:1–18; Nehemiah's prayer in Nehemiah 1:5–11; and Jesus's prayers in Matthew 26:36–46, 27:45–46, and Luke 23:34, 46.

Sacred Perspectives

If a friend receives recognition that you desire, do you struggle with envy? What if a co-worker is promoted or given some special privilege that you think you deserve more? For many women, envy and comparison are natural responses, although we almost never talk about it. When was the last time you heard someone request prayer for the sin of envy? Yet Solomon points out the destructive nature of envy in Proverbs 14:30: "A heart at peace gives life to the body, but envy rots the bones."

Leadership expert John Maxwell distinguished himself in his denomination as the youngest pastor to be elected to a national office and to average more than a thousand in attendance at his church. Sadly, he writes that he was also the loneliest person in his denomination. When he failed, people were there for him, but when he succeeded, he and his wife celebrated alone (*Winning with People*, 209).

James instructs us not to "harbor bitter envy and selfish ambition" in our hearts, and he insists that envy is a source of "disorder and every evil practice" (James 3:14, 16). Paul writes about envious people in our passage this week. They pitted themselves against Paul, and we don't want to be like them. Until we deal with our jealousy and envy, peace will evade us and conflict is likely.

While some women battle comparison and envy, other women battle a critical spirit. They lack a long-suffering heart toward people who disappoint them. Their judgmental attitudes can also weaken the church and cause strife and division. In our text this week, Paul counsels both groups, showing us how to work toward health and unity in our faith communities, despite various kinds of opposition.

Read Philippians 1:12–30.

27

1. According to Paul, what good is resulting from his imprisonment (1:12)?

2. What is one specific example Paul mentions in verse 13? Why do you think this has happened?

3. Are you in close proximity to non-Christians due to work, school, or family obligations? If so, what opportunities might these situations provide? How might you serve as Christ's ambassador there?

4. How have other Christ-followers been affected by Paul's imprisonment (1:14)? In your opinion, why? If you have ever observed or experienced a similar situation, please share.

5. When Christians find themselves in difficult situations, their admirable responses often make Christ look good. Can you recall a difficult experience in your life that God used to "advance the gospel"? If so, please relate it to the group.

6. Into what two categories do Paul's fellow ministers fit? What does Paul say are the motives of each? (1:15–17)

DIGGING DEEPER

To learn more of Joseph's saga from the pit to the palace and beyond, read Genesis 37–50. Why is he the poster child displaying the beauty of God's redemptive story?

7. How difficult is it to discern other people's motives? Do you think it is harder to discern motives or to judge false doctrine? Support your answer.

Be generous of spirit. . . . You will be much better off if you view the situation as: "If she became a vice president, then there's hope for me too." Such an optimistic attitude allows you to be truly happy with someone else's success. Rather than feeling it's her gain and your loss, it's better to view the situation as her gain and inspiration for you.
—Pat Heim and Susan Murphy
(*In the Company of Women*, 184)

8. What was Paul's attitude toward false teachers (see 2 Corinthians 11:13–15; Galatians 1:8; Philippians 3:2)? In light of his attitude, does Paul believe those who "preach Christ out of envy and rivalry" (1:15) are false teachers? Why or why not? What is the lesson for us?

9. Paul realizes that some Christians envy his position and prestige (1:15). How would you have felt if you were Paul? Why do you think he was able to ignore their envy? What are the lessons for us?

· More than 90 percent of women of different social strata claim that envy and jealousy toward other women colors their lives.
· 80 percent of women say they have encountered jealousy in other females since they were in grade school.
· 90 percent of women in diverse jobs report that competition in the workplace is primarily between women, rather than between women and men.
· More than 65 percent of interviewees said that they were jealous of their best friend or sister.
—Susan Shapiro Barash
(from her research resulting in her book *Tripping the Prom Queen*, 12)

10. Why do you think Paul is more accepting of impure motives than incorrect doctrine?

11. What is Paul's attitude toward those who support him as well as those who want to discredit him? Why? (1:18)

To learn more about ways to navigate female envy, jealousy, and rivalry, read *Leading Women Who Wound* by Sue Edwards and Kelley Mathews (Moody Publishers, 2009).

12. What is your attitude toward modern-day ministers with questionable motives? Toward those who may want to discredit you? Discuss. (No names, please.) What can we learn from Paul?

Paul's confinement has limited his opportunities to travel, plant churches, preach, and encourage his dear brothers and sisters throughout the Roman Empire who now share his love for Jesus. As a result, Christians have stepped in to fill the leadership gap, some who want to honor Paul and obey God's call, others who were jealous of Paul and sense the chance to win influence for themselves. Paul rejoices over both, refusing to allow these circumstances to squelch his joy. He models love, even when people disappoint him and don't meet his expectations. Next he shares his perspectives on life and death.

13. As Paul faces possible impending execution, what are his primary sources of strength? What does he believe will be the end result of his imprisonment? (1:19)

14. Specifically, what are the two possible outcomes? What is Paul's main concern as he faces an uncertain future? (1:19–21)

15. How does he feel concerning each possibility? Why does he want to live? Why does he want to die? (1:22–24)

16. Who will benefit most if Paul is released? Why does he look forward to that possible end? (1:24–26)

17. Paul begins verse 27 with the words, "Whatever happens." How does he face the future (1:4, 18b; 2:18; 3:1a; 4:4, 10a)?

18. Can you honestly say with Paul, "to live is Christ and to die is gain" (1:21)? How do you think it is possible to have Paul's perspective? What are the benefits of living life with this perspective?

Thus far in this letter, Paul has prepared his friends for the possible sudden news that he had been executed, comforting and consoling them by assuring them that he is joyful, whatever happens, and that he is certain God will use even these circumstances for good. Now beginning in verse 27, Paul instructs the Philippians.

19. What phrases in verses 27–30 suggest that the Philippians are facing strong opposition?

In my early years, I regularly battled insecurity. My mother believed that constant criticism was good for a girl, but her negativity backfired. By my mid-twenties I was an insecure, depressed mess. And one unintended consequence of feeling less than everyone else is a gnawing envy when others thrive. Then I met Jesus, accepted his unconditional love, and began to grow in my faith. But jealousy, that green-eyed monster, kept after me. I wanted to rejoice when others did well, but often my sin nature would rear its ugly head when a friend was asked to speak for a group instead of me or their child was honored with a trophy that I felt my child deserved. It's taken some years, but once I named the sin and dug it out by its roots, I was able to wholeheartedly delight in others' accomplishments and blessings. Now I realize that we are all designed to play a small part in God's work, and he decides what part we each play. When we labor together, encouraging one another, our Father's work will be accomplished. If you struggle with envy, jealousy, or even the kind of critical spirit Paul talks about in this passage, savor Paul's instructions and cooperate with the Holy Spirit within you to win the battle over envy, jealousy, or a critical spirit. Together, you can experience victory! —Sue

DIGGING DEEPER

Paul revealed more on unity and its powerful impact on a watching world in Ephesians 2:11–22 and 3:1–13. Wring out these passages and summarize how diverse people become one in the bond of Christian love.

My mother is not the only one who relies on singing in times of struggle and pain. As I have traveled with my husband to meet persecuted Christians around the world, I have heard countless believers who share her experience: it helps to sing through the night.
—Anneke Companjen (*Singing Through the Night*, 16)

20. What does Paul tell them to do as they face opposition (1:27–28a)?

21. What effect does the unity of Christians have on those who oppose the cause of Christ (1:27–28)?

22. How critical is unity in Christendom today? What difference could a unified universal church make in the world? What can you do to encourage unity?

. . . .

Envy and Jealousy: Barriers to Unity (*6:45 minutes*).

. . . .

23. See Philippians 1:29–30 and 3:10; what is one "privilege" of being a Christian?

24. We aren't exactly sure what "struggle" Paul is referring to in verse 30. What are some of the possibilities (see 2 Corinthians 11:23–33; 12:7–10)?

25. Have you or anyone you know ever suffered for the cause of Christ? If so, share the incident with your group.

26. How can we prepare now to glorify Christ if we are called to endure persecution for our faith?

DIGGING DEEPER

To prepare yourself for challenges, even persecutions, that may present themselves for believers in the future, read 1 Peter or Jesus's letters to the seven churches in Revelation. Record what you learn or what encouragement you receive from these passages. (After this study of Philippians, consider studying Sue's *1 Peter: Discovering Encouragement in Troubling Times* and/or *Daniel: Discovering the Courage to Stand for Your Faith*. Both studies are designed to help Christian women thrive regardless of difficult circumstances.)

An Inspiring Example | LESSON 4

Humility and self-sacrifice were not popular in the Roman world where Paul lived and they are not popular in our world either. But God highly values these qualities and encourages all his children to develop and display them. These qualities are foundations for unity, health, and strength in God's family and in our personal lives. They help us band together and overcome struggles and opposition. They woo others to seek God and join the body of Christ. They light up a dark world. And as we love and serve each other, we experience joy, grace, and fulfilling work.

I want to be humble and think of others before I think of myself, but, if I'm honest, it's hard. Too often my first inclination is to think of myself. I realize my error and correct it. I make headway and then fall back. I'm much better than I used to be, but I'm not there yet.

I need the encouragement and support of others. I need beautiful examples as incentives. I need constant reminders, and a loving God to work within me. So do you. And God provides all these for us. One way he provides help is through his Word, and particularly through portions of Scripture like Philippians chapter 2. Lessons 4 and 5 focus on passages that paint beautiful pictures of humility and self-sacrifice, models to inspire and motivate us. Come see, learn, and imitate, for God's glory and your joy.

Read Philippians 2:1–16.

1. In verse 1, Paul lists blessings Christians enjoy as God's children in community together. What are they? (Note: The word "if" in Greek is a first class condition, expressing the assumption that each statement is true, and therefore is better translated "since.")

OPTIONAL

Memorize Philippians 2:3–4

Do nothing out of selfish ambition or vain conceit. Rather, in humility value others above yourselves, not looking to your own interests but each of you to the interests of the others.

In what sense have Christians been united with Christ (Philippians 2:1)? Why is this such a great encouragement (see Romans 6:1–14; Galatians 2:20)?

This is a call to wake up to the fact that we can never realize the likeness of Christ by ourselves alone; we will never transform the world as individuals; we will never discover fullness of life in Christ if we stay solo. We are distinct as people of God because we were made to live in dependence on the head and interdependently with the diverse parts of the body. Community that is distinctively Christian will have group dynamics that are healthy. But it will embrace more. Community that is distinctively Christian will host the presence of God in the midst of it! It is God himself who makes community possible. His presence is catalytic to the experiencing of togetherness beyond human endeavor.

—Julie Gorman (*Community That Is Christian*, 12)

Every day I can choose humility, acknowledging your great value to God—he died for you! I can recognize his sovereign right to direct your life and to gift you with blessings he withholds from me. I can acknowledge my own sinful nature that cost Christ his life and admit loudly, and often, "I am no better and no more deserving than anyone else on this planet!"

—Jan Winebrenner (*Intimate Faith*, 29)

2. Can you remember a specific time when you experienced and enjoyed any of the blessings listed in 2:1? If so, what happened? Please share.

3. Paul asks the Philippians to do something in response to God's marvelous blessings. What will complete Paul's joy and delight God as well (2:2; 1:27)?

4. Disunity, dissension, and disharmony can destroy a church, family, community, or nation. What does Paul advise as an antidote (2:3–4)?

5. Discuss the differences between self-absorption, self-care, and self-sacrifice.

6. Does considering "others above yourselves" (2:3) mean that everyone else is superior to you in every way? Does this concept negate your value? If not, what do you think Paul means by this idea?

7. Why is it difficult for many people to live a life of self-sacrifice, "valuing others above" themselves? Do you struggle to live out this virtue?

8. What are some ways you have observed people looking out for the best interests of others? How would our world and your life be different if this was common practice?

Now Paul paints a picture of the Person who best exemplifies this kind of life. Verses 6–11 are known as the *kenosis* (the emptying), reflecting grand and mysterious christological truths. Savor each word. Ask God to guide you through this divine literary masterpiece and open up realities that you may not have seen before.

9. Who models humility and sacrifice more than anyone else who ever lived?

DIGGING DEEPER

Analyze and synthesize the following passages:
1 Corinthians 8:6;
2 Corinthians 8:9; Colossians 1:16–17. How do they complement the *kenosis*, Philippians 2:6–11?

10. What is the command in 2:5? What is the purpose of the *kenosis* passage?

11. Who is Christ Jesus (2:6a; see also Colossians 1:15; Hebrews 1:2–3; John 1:1–3, 14)?

12. Is it possible for us to possess the same mind-set and attitude as Christ Jesus (1 Corinthians 2:15–16)? In what sense might this be true? In what sense does this seem impossible (Isaiah 55:8)?

13. What are Jesus's rights and privileges as God (2:6a)? Name as many as you can.

14. What was Jesus's attitude toward those rights and privileges (2:6; Hebrews 12:2–3)? Was this attitude voluntary or forced?

15. What do you think is the meaning of 2:7, "he made himself nothing"? See also Luke 2:11–12.

16. What else did he do (2:8; Hebrews 12:2)?

17. What did Jesus explain to his disciples in Luke 9:23–25? What do you think he meant?

18. What is your "cross"? When have you denied yourself or given up your rights?

19. What was God the Father's response to this supreme example of humility and self-sacrifice (2:9–11)?

 A Grand Mystery and a Glorious Example (*10:50 minutes*).

In Philippians 2:12–13, Paul interweaves the mystery of God's indwelling enablement with man's efforts and choices. (Note: The Philippians were not to work "for" salvation but to work "out" the salvation they already possessed.)

20. Why does Paul praise the Philippians? What is the command? (2:12)

21. What part do we play as we "work out" our salvation (2:12)? What part does God play (2:13)?

22. Specifically, what is God doing "in order to fulfill his good purpose" in your life right now? How can you more fully cooperate with him?

It is difficult for us, after so many Christian centuries during which the cross has been venerated as a sacred symbol, to realize the unspeakable horror and disgust that the mention or indeed the very thought of the cross provoked. . . . In polite Roman society the word "cross" was an obscenity, not to be uttered in conversation. Even when a man was sentenced to death by crucifixion, an archaic formula was used that avoided the pronouncing of the four-letter word—as it was in Latin (*crux*). This utterly vile form of punishment was that which Jesus endured, and by enduring it he turned the shameful instrument of torture into the object of his followers' proudest boast. "May I never boast," said Paul . . . "except in the cross of our Lord Jesus Christ" (Gal. 6:14)— an incomprehensible turning upside down of all accepted values of his day.
—F. F. Bruce (*Philippians*, 71-72)

DIGGING DEEPER

In Luke 14:7–11, Jesus told a parable instructing us to follow his example. What can you learn from the parable? What are some specific ways you can "take the lowest place" so that God can exalt you in time?

Paul has exhorted the Philippians to seek a spirit of unity, only possible through an attitude of humility and self-sacrifice. And he has instructed them to cooperate with God who is working to enable them to be Christ-like. He concludes with a beautiful picture of who they are becoming.

23. What will foster disunity and disharmony? What is the instruction in 2:14?

24. Can you relate a time when you saw complaining and arguing destroy unity? (No names, please.)

25. Do you complain and argue often? If so, when and why? What is the result?

26. If the Philippians take Paul's commands to heart, what will result (2:15–16a)?

27. What do you think it means to "shine . . . like stars in the sky" (2:15) and to "hold firmly to the word of life" (2:16; see Matthew 5:14–16; 2 Peter 1:19)? What are some ways to do this?

28. Why was it vital that the Philippian church be mature, unified, and "shining" in Philippi? Why is it vital that you "shine" in your world today?

29. What does the Holy Spirit want you to apply from Lesson 4? Create a plan to act on what you know God wants you to do this week. Expect God to help you as you lie down in his hands.

More Inspiring Examples and a Warning

We saw in lesson 4 that Jesus is the supreme example of self-sacrifice and humility (2:6–8). I'm in awe of his beauty and perfection. But to emulate these qualities in my own life, I also need examples of ordinary people, like my friends Kathy, Vickie, Joye, Mike, and George. If I were writing a letter or sending an email to friends who needed to see *Jesus with skin on*, I'd tell them about the friends I just mentioned. Over the years I've observed their lives and, oh, the stories I could tell, wonderful stories of them putting others first, considering others more valuable than themselves, of taking on the nature of a servant. In our passage today, Paul provided these kinds of examples for the Philippians and for us.

> Paul did not set out deliberately to present three examples of the same self-denouncing attitude "as that of Christ Jesus" (v. 5). But in fact that is what he has done. His own readiness to have his martyrdom credited to the spiritual account of his Philippian friends, Timothy's unselfish service to Paul and genuine concern for other Christians, Epaphroditus's devotion to his mission at great risk to his health and (as it might have been) to his life—all these display the unselfconscious care for others . . . reinforced by the powerful example of Christ's self-emptying. (F. F. Bruce, *Philippians*, 98)

In years past, I tended to skim over Bible passages full of names and personal greetings or information, assuming these sections had little to teach me. But I've come to understand that these parts offer "fly on the wall" lessons on relationships that often reflect authentic biblical community, a quality we sometimes miss because of our individualistic tendencies. Listen carefully to tender accolades and expressions of Christlike love, and imitate, sister, imitate.

Read Philippians 2:17–30.

OPTIONAL

Memorize Romans 12:5

In Christ we, though many, form one body, and each member belongs to all the others.

Paul speaks of himself as being "poured" out like a drink offering. When someone offered a costly sacrifice to God, they could also pour out a drink offering over the sacrifice or on the ground nearby. This was a special thanksgiving or praise offering to God. In verse 17, Paul views his possible death as a drink offering to complement the sacrifice he sees exhibited in the lives of the Philippians.

THE EXAMPLE OF PAUL

1. In Romans 12:1, Paul makes a plea to the Roman Christians. What does he ask them to do? How is he a living example of the plea in Philippians 2:17–18?

2. What is Paul's attitude toward self-sacrifice and his possible death by decapitation (2:17–18)?

DIGGING DEEPER

Read and dissect 1 Corinthians 15 for an in-depth study of what happens when we die. How has this study soothed your fears about dying and helped you better understand Paul's ability to rejoice even in his own death?

3. How do you think one learns to think about death like Paul? Study the following verses and write out what you learn about death: Hebrews 2:14; 2 Timothy 1:10; Revelation 21:4.

THE EXAMPLE OF TIMOTHY

It is interesting that he doesn't say "Timothy is a wonderful teacher," or even "Timothy is a very devout and holy man," but, "Timothy will genuinely care about you." The definition Paul seems to adopt for a good pastor—and the implication is that he himself was like this—has more to do with sheer unselfish love than anything to do with the person themselves.

—Tom Wright
(*Paul for Everyone*, 109)

4. Paul habitually mentored young men, preparing them to carry on God's work after he departed. One of them, Timothy, served as Paul's constant companion in Rome, but Paul hoped to send him to Philippi for a visit. Why (2:19)?

5. From 2:19–24, what can you glean about the relationship between Paul and Timothy? How did Timothy exhibit sacrificial love?

THE EXAMPLE OF EPAPHRODITUS

6. How does Paul feel about Epaphroditus (2:25, 29–30)?

7. Why is he there with Paul? What is his ministry? (2:25; Philippians 4:18)

8. Why is Epaphroditus distressed (2:26)?

9. Why is Paul sending him back to Philippi (2:27–28)?

10. According to 2:25–30, how did Epaphroditus exhibit genuine Christian love and service?

11. Paul included many details about these two fellow servants in the letter. What does this tell you about Paul? About Timothy and Epaphroditus? About the Philippians? How might you apply these lessons to your own life?

The disciplines of humility and submission train us to live joyfully, peacefully, in the realm of divine mystery. They work to strengthen the ligaments and tendons of our knees, often only by "painful effort," until we can bow before God, bending low in the shadow of his transcendence, accepting the unknown of this life without argument or resistance.
—Jan Winebrenner
(*Intimate Faith*, 20–21)

Community is, of course, central to Christianity at every life stage—after all, the very life of the Triune God tells us that we are persons only when we are in communion with one another.
—Lauren Winner
(*Mudhouse Sabbath*, 103)

The Rich Gift of Relationships (*11:13 minutes*).

Read Philippians 3:1–11.

12. Considering some of the bad news in this letter (Paul's imprisonment and impending execution, Epaphroditus's recent severe illness, the apparent persecution of the church), how can Paul tell the Philippians to rejoice? What does he tell them to rejoice in? (3:1) What do you think this means?

13. Is it possible to have joy in the midst of sorrowful circumstances? Has this ever been your experience? If so, when? Please share.

In these verses, Paul warns the Philippians about legalistic Jews called Judaizers. They insisted that Gentiles had to be circumcised and follow the law to become Christians. If these false teachers had succeeded, they would have turned Christianity into nothing more than a sect of Judaism.

14. In your opinion, why doesn't Paul mind repeating himself on this subject (3:1b)? Why do you sometimes repeat yourself?

Jews often referred to Gentiles as dogs—not a term of endearment. In the first century, these animals were not cuddly house pets but wild, disgusting animals that roamed the streets and threatened people's safety.

15. What does he call the Judaizers in verse 2?

16. What does Paul mean when he says, "For it is we who are the circumcision" in verse 3 (see also Romans 2:28–29)?

17. What characterizes those who are circumcised in their hearts (3:3)?

18. If anyone were to put confidence in legalistic Judaism, why would Paul be eminently qualified (3:4–6)? What privileges and status do you think Paul enjoyed when he was a Pharisee?

19. When Paul abandoned Judaism and came to faith in Christ, what would he have lost? What did he think about this loss (3:7–8)? What do some people lose today when they come to faith?

20. What did he gain (3:8b–9; Romans 3:21–26)?

DIGGING DEEPER

The Judaizers were Jewish believers who taught that to be saved one must also keep the Mosaic Law. Study Acts 15 where Paul and Barnabas confront the Judaizers before the Council of Jerusalem. How did the council's decision impact the future of Christianity?

DIGGING DEEPER

Learn more about Paul's former life from Acts 7:54–8:3; 22:1–5; and Galatians 1:13–14.

The Judaizers were also spreading their false doctrine in the churches in Galatia. Discuss Paul's related warnings in Galatians 1:6–9 and 3:1–11.

I rejected the church for a time because I found so little grace there. I returned because I found grace nowhere else.
—Philip Yancey (*What's So Amazing About Grace?*, 16)

We are cruel to ourselves if we try to live in this world without knowing about the God whose world it is and who runs it. The world becomes a strange, mad, painful place, and life in it a disappointing and unpleasant business, for those who do not know about God. Disregard the study of God, and you sentence yourself to stumble and blunder through life blindfolded, as it were, with no sense of direction and no understanding of what surrounds you. This way you can waste your life and lose your soul.
—J. I. Packer
(*Knowing God*, 14–15)

21. Discuss the complicated relationship of good works and faith (see Ephesians 2:8–10; Luke 23:39–43; James 2:14–26)?

22. Do you tend to attempt to earn God's favor by doing good works? Why or why not? Why do you think Paul is so adamant about the doctrine of salvation by faith alone in Christ alone?

23. What does Paul say he wants to know in 3:10? What do you think he means by these statements (see also Ephesians 1:17–23; James 1:2–4)?

24. What results from our coming to faith and "knowing" Christ (3:11)?

25. Do you "know" Christ in this sense? What do Jeremiah 9:23–24 and John 17:3 reveal about knowing Jesus intimately? What difference has an intimate relationship with Jesus made in your life?

26. Paul describes resurrection power in Ephesians 1:18–20. What kind of power is he talking about? Can you share a time when you saw this power at work? What resulted?

God is knowable, and He does want to be known. . . . The [Greek] word know [in Philippians 3:10] . . . does not refer to a casual acquaintance either. It is the kind of knowledge that comes through living contact and personal relationship.
—Richard L. Strauss (*The Joy of Knowing God*, 11)

27. How do you feel about Paul's desire to share in the sufferings of Christ? In what sense would this experience be frightening? In what sense would this be an honor?

28. What truth is the Holy Spirit impressing on you right now, and what do you plan to do about it?

The Courageous Pursuit | LESSON 6

All great classics, whether captured on pages of books or unfolding as masterful films, embrace a quest, an adventure, a beautiful story, a pursuit. Our spiritual lives are nothing less than a great odyssey. Once we choose to accept God's invitation to know and love him, we each begin a race full of drama, intrigue, and wonder as we journey through life with Christ as our energy, our guide, and our goal. As we go, we discover how impossible it is to run the race without him and how grand and wonderful he really is. We also discover that as we finally understand his all-encompassing role in our lives, we become more aware of our own inadequacies.

As Paul grew in spiritual maturity, he too became increasingly aware of his own inadequacies. In 1 Corinthians, one of Paul's earlier letters, he stated that he was the least of the apostles (15:9). Then in Ephesians, a later letter, he spoke of himself as the least of all the Lord's people (3:8). Finally, in one of his last letters, 1 Timothy, he called himself the worst of all sinners (1:15). In Philippians 3:12–4:1 this chief sinner exhorts us to "press on" to spiritual maturity in our individual races, and he shows us how.

Read Philippians 3:12–4:1.

1. To review, list Paul's goals in his spiritual race (3:10). Are these the end goals of your Christian life? Why or why not?

2. What is Paul's attitude toward his own spiritual maturity in 3:12–13? How do you feel about the fact that he admits his limitations and inadequacies?

OPTIONAL

Memorize Philippians 3:13b–14

One thing I do: Forgetting what is behind and straining toward what is ahead, I press on toward the goal to win the prize for which God has called me heavenward in Christ Jesus.

OPTIONAL ACTIVITY

To prepare for this lesson, consider viewing the film *Chariots of Fire* by yourself or with your group. Discuss the various ways Eric Liddell honored God by the way he ran and lived. How did he serve as a model for us as we run our spiritual race?

If your translation only addresses "brothers" in 3:13, 17, and 4:1, remember that this Greek word is gender neutral and today would be more accurately translated "brothers and sisters."

DIGGING DEEPER

Write a paragraph or two exploring the difference between perfection and excellence.

3. Do you struggle to admit your own limitations and inadequacies? Why or why not?

4. How do you relate to Christians who project an image of perfection personified?

 It's a Marathon! (*8:32 minutes*).

5. Both Paul and the Philippians are enduring great struggles at this time. In 3:12 and 14 Paul writes, "I press on." What is he attempting to teach the Philippians and all believers by these words? What is God teaching us through our trials and adversity (see Romans 5:3–4; James 1:2–4; 2 Thessalonians 1:3–4)?

6. Do you "press on" or do you quickly give up when the going gets tough? Share your related struggles and/or victories.

7. Phrases such as "straining toward what is ahead" (3:13) and "I press on toward the goal" (3:14) suggest athletic events, popular in ancient Greece. Other New Testament passages also use athletics to illustrate spiritual truths. Look up the following verses and rephrase them briefly in your own words. If you are a runner, share any related insight.

1 Corinthians 9:24–27

Hebrews 12:1–3

2 Timothy 4:7–8

8. In several passages related to athletics, a prize or crown is mentioned as the reward for a race well run. Read 1 Corinthians 3:8–9; 2 John 8; and Revelation 22:12. From these passages, how will Christians be rewarded in heaven?

To learn more about believers' rewards at the *bema* seat, read *Your Eternal Reward* by Erwin W. Lutzer (Moody Publishers, 1998), or *The Bema, A Story about the Judgment Seat of Christ* by Tim Stevenson (Fair Haven Publications, 2000).

9. What is one reward all Christians have already received (1 John 5:11–12; John 5:24)?

10. Runners must keep their eyes fixed on the finish line or risk losing the race. What is one mistake in growing spiritually that could greatly hinder you (3:13; 2 Peter 1:9)?

The analogy is clear. In this race called life, we are to face forward, anticipating what lies ahead, ever stretching and reaching, making life a passionate, adventurous quest. Life was never meant to be a passive coexistence with enemy forces as we await our heavenly home. Let me pause here and ask you three direct questions: Have you left the past—I mean fully moved on beyond it? Are you making progress—some kind of deliberate progress with your life? Do you passionately pursue some dream—some specific goal? . . . There is something wonderfully exciting about reaching into the future with excited anticipation, and those who pursue new adventures through life stay younger, think better, and laugh louder!
—Charles R. Swindoll
(*Laugh Again*, 148–49)

11. Do you tend to dwell on past mistakes and failures? How could this prevent you from pressing on? What can you do to "forget what is behind" (see 1 John 1:8–9; Psalm 103:10–14)?

12. According to 3:12–15, what are the marks of a mature Christian?

13. How does God deal with those who are "immature" (3:15)? Has this ever happened to you? If so, when?

14. What is the command in verse 16? What has God already provided for you? How do you live up to his current provisions?

15. What situation may have made Paul think a strong Christian model was necessary for the Philippians (3:17–18)?

16. The people Paul described in 3:19 are radically different from the Judaizers he referred to in 3:2. How are they different? (To review Paul's teachings on the Judaizers, see Galatians 2:15–16.) Why are the ideas of the people in verse 19 also a threat to the Philippians as they run their individual spiritual races?

17. Do you struggle more with legalism or license as you run your spiritual race? How might each slow you down?

18. Paul exhorts the Philippians to follow wise examples as they run their race. What is the importance of having a "model" (3:17) or someone to look up to in the Christian life? Has anyone been your model? Have you been someone else's? Please share either experience and its value in your life.

19. What danger might there be in having a model? How can you protect yourself from this danger?

My Dad served as a Coast Guard officer for thirty years, which meant that our family was patriotic to the core—flag waving, apple pie, Fourth of July patriotic. I love my country. But recently I sense that my country doesn't love me. My Christian values make me radically different from so many of my fellow North Americans. I'm experiencing a mammoth adjustment. I fret, I grieve, I'm angry. I realize that I've wed the two: my citizenship in my country and in God's kingdom. I never had to choose before. But one benefit is that for the first time, I better understand first-century Christians. The people in the Bible never lived in a land where their values were honored. Neither have most believers throughout history. Why did I think God owed me a nation where my values as a believer were respected? As a result, my race takes on new dimensions, but God knows and he's carrying me forward. If you share these sentiments, let him carry you too. —Sue

20. The "enemies of the cross of Christ" focus their minds on earthly things (3:18–19). In contrast, where should spiritual runners focus their minds? Where is our citizenship? (3:20; see also 1 Peter 1:1)

21. How do you view your citizenship in the country where you live? Are you more loyal to that country than you are to God's kingdom? How does the decline or the prosperity of your nation of origin affect your citizenship in God's kingdom? Discuss.

22. In 3:20–21, Paul gives the Philippians a marvelous incentive for staying away from the "enemies of the cross of Christ" and their lifestyle. Discuss what the Philippians, as well as all Christians, have to look forward to.

23. Paul says our earthly bodies will be transformed into bodies like Christ's resurrected body. What can you learn about this new body from the following passages?

John 20:19–20

Luke 24:39–43

1 Corinthians 15:42–49

Romans 8:29–30

24. How do Paul and the Philippians feel about Christ's coming kingdom (3:20)? How do you feel?

This is the greatest challenge of the letter: that the Christians in Philippi, whether or not they were themselves Roman citizens (some probably were, many probably weren't), would think out what it means to give their primary allegiance not to Rome but to heaven, not to Caesar but to Jesus— and to trust that Jesus would in due time bring the life and rule of heaven to bear on the whole world, themselves included.

—Tom Wright
(*Paul for Everyone*, 127)

25. In 4:1, Paul tells the Philippians to "stand firm in the Lord in this way." What has he told them in 3:12–21 that will help them "stand firm"? Which of these instructions helps you in your life right now? Why or how?

26. Evaluate the pace of your race. What might be tying you down? Are you looking back? Down? Around? What have you learned from Paul's instructions concerning his race to help you with yours? How will you get back on track and finish well?

A Harmonious Peace | LESSON 7

OPTIONAL

Depending on your personal needs this week, memorize one of these powerful, mind-molding verses from Philippians 4

Rejoice in the Lord always. I will say it again: Rejoice! Let your gentleness be evident to all. The Lord is near. (4:4–5)

Do not be anxious about anything, but in every situation, by prayer and petition, with thanksgiving, present your requests to God. And the peace of God, which transcends all understanding, will guard your hearts and your minds in Christ Jesus. (4:6–7)

Whatever is true, whatever is noble, whatever is right, whatever is pure, whatever is lovely, whatever is admirable—if anything is excellent or praiseworthy—think about such things. (4:8)

Conflict is inevitable, even among Christians. Unfortunately, few Christians are skilled peacemakers. Jesus's instructions on what to do in a conflict is one of the most neglected passages of Scripture. Families implode, leadership teams crumble, and churches split because of the lack of conflict resolution skills.

I'm no exception. In my forty-plus years of marriage, my husband and I worked hard to learn how to handle conflict in our family. I'm an energetic, type A, visionary-teacher, goal oriented, get-it-done-now leader. He's a laid-back engineer, gifted as a prison ministry evangelist, always ready to stop and chat, with a tender desire to take his time and serve others. Early in our marriage, our different temperaments and gift mixes butted heads often. But we learned to pursue peace using biblical guidelines because we love each other and Jesus. You can too, if you are willing to submit yourself to biblical mandates—like the ones we are about to learn.

In my thirty-plus years of ministry, I've experienced two serious conflicts with other women leaders. The first one almost took me out of ministry. I was ultimately exonerated, but badly bruised. I did not know how to work through the crisis, but afterward I was determined to learn more and to help others. Most Christians are as unprepared for conflict as I was. I handled the second one better than the first, but I still made mistakes. Since then, I've worked hard to hone my skills and God has enabled me to handle the few conflicts I've experienced with grace and expertise. I'm amazed at how much better the process goes when we follow Jesus's instructions, provided we are dealing with healthy people. Even Jesus had his Judas.

In this lesson, we will focus on a serious conflict in Philippi and then learn what to do when conflict explodes in our lives.

Read Philippians 4:2–9.

To learn more about how women respond emotionally to conflict, how they perceive conflict, and even how they may practice conflict, read Sue Edwards's book, coauthored with Kelley Mathews, *Leading Women Who Wound* (Moody Publishers, 2009).

1. Two women leaders in the church were embroiled in a serious conflict (4:2). How do you know it was serious? What do you learn about their former relationship with Paul from 4:3? Why might this situation have grieved Paul deeply?

2. What did Paul first suggest as a way to settle the disagreement (4:2)? What was his second suggestion? Who did Paul enlist to help them (4:3)? What are the lessons for us?

Jesus taught us exactly what to do to achieve harmony in our relationships. Read Matthew 18:15–17. (The person referred to in this passage is a fellow believer, male or female.)

Avoid godless chatter, because those who indulge in it will become more and more ungodly. Their teaching will spread like gangrene.
—2 Timothy 2:16–17

3. If you are wounded by or angry with another believer, what does Jesus tell you to do (18:15)? How many people should be involved at this stage?

4. In a conflict, are you eager to call a friend or tell a loved one about it? Why is it difficult not to include others? What can happen if you involve others in this first step?

5. What is the goal of Matthew 18:15? Why is it so important that conflict be dealt with at this stage in the disagreement?

6. Have you ever practiced Jesus's command in 18:15? If so, how did you feel? What happened? (No names, please.)

7. In reality, the wisdom of 18:15 is often ignored. In your opinion, why?

8. If your conflict is not resolved by practicing what is taught in 18:15, what is the next step (18:16)? Who would qualify as a "witness"? Why do you think Jesus says you may include more than one?

9. What usually happens to the dynamics of a conversation when others besides the people in conflict are present? Have you ever seen this occur? If so, how were witnesses helpful?

10. If the conflict is still not resolved, what does Jesus advise you to do (18:17)? What do you think this means? Practically, how might this look?

Instead of wanting to persuade and get your way, you want to understand what has happened from the other person's point of view, explain your point of view, share and understand feelings, and work together to figure out a way to manage the problem going forward. . . . Changing our stance means inviting the other person into the conversation with us, to help us figure things out. If we're going to achieve our purpose, we have lots we need to learn from them and lots they need to learn from us. We need to have a learning conversation.
—Douglas Stone, Bruce Patton, and Sheila Heen
(*Difficult Conversations*, 16–17)

The mere presence of an audience (including psychological presence) motivates bargainers to seek positive, and avoid negative, evaluation—especially when the audience is important to the bargainers. The external audience helps keep the bargaining process honest. The effect of the negotiator's behavior before a watching world provides a check-and-balance system so that grave injustices are less likely to occur.
—Kenneth Gangel and Samuel Canine (*Communication and Conflict Management*, 216)

11. If the conflict is still not resolved, Jesus tells you to treat the other party as you would a tax collector or a pagan. How did Jesus treat tax collectors and pagans (see Matthew 11:19)? What would that relationship look like? How would it be different from what it was before?

12. How might a more fervent practice of Matthew 18:15–17 result in more harmony in the church? In the home? In the office? In school? In the community?

13. How can you personally prepare right now to consistently practice Matthew 18:15–17? Be specific. Come up with as many practical suggestions as you can.

 Become a Relational Peacemaker (*9:47 minutes*).

14. Paul reiterates the theme of the letter in Philippians 4:4. What is the theme? Why do you think he continues to emphasize this message right after pleading with the Philippians to settle their disagreements?

15. What is Paul's request in 4:5? Define this trait. What do you think Paul means by this word?

16. This trait was used to describe Jesus in Matthew 11:28–30. How might this trait improve the likelihood of a peaceful resolution in a conflict?

17. This trait is one of the fruits of the Spirit. What do Galatians 5:22–26 and 6:1 teach you about peacemaking?

I have often wondered, that persons who make boast of professing the Christian religion, namely love, joy, peace, temperance, and charity to all men, should quarrel with such rancorous animosity, and display daily towards one another such bitter hatred, that this, rather than the virtues they claim, is the readiest criteria of their faith.
—Benedict de Spinoza, Jewish philosopher (*A Theological-Political Treatise and a Political Treatise*)

18. Solomon knew the power of this trait. What do you learn from Proverbs 15:1 and 25:15?

DIGGING DEEPER

Even if you are caught in an unfair conflict, what does Peter instruct you to do (1 Peter 3:13–16)?

19. Do you know anyone who personifies gentleness? If so, describe them. If not, describe what you imagine it should look like.

20. Do you display gentleness when you are entangled in a conflict? If so, how did you learn to respond this way? If not, how might you develop this trait, preparing you for future conflicts?

Conflicts often threaten a relationship. As a result, fear, anxiety, anger, frustration—all these emotions—naturally accompany an argument. Now Paul tells us how to overcome negative emotions that often sabotage a healthy peace process. Seldom do we study this passage in the context of peacemaking, but that is the issue Paul is presenting in 4:2–5. Certainly the principles can apply to other situations, but the immediate context involved conflict.

21. How do you usually feel when a conflict erupts?

Carefully analyze 4:6–7 below. Consider how this passage might help you reign in the runaway emotions often experienced in conflict. Underline the commands. Circle the promise.

Do not be anxious about anything, but in every situation, by prayer and petition, with thanksgiving, present your requests to God. And the peace of God, which transcends all understanding, will guard your hearts and your minds in Christ Jesus.

22. What is the first thing Paul tells us to do when we are experiencing conflict (4:6–7)? How do you typically pray while involved in a conflict? What kinds of prayers would lead to a healthier peacemaking process?

23. Meditate on John 14:27. How might the peace of God in your heart and mind help you as you enter into a healthy peacemaking process with another Christian?

24. Why do you think Paul asks you to pray with thanksgiving in a conflict? What can you be thankful for? In what sense can peacemaking be an opportunity and a blessing?

25. Can you share with the group a time when you experienced the truth of 4:6–7? What happened? (No names, please.)

> Peace I leave with you; my peace I give you. I do not give to you as the world gives. Do not let your hearts be troubled and do not be afraid.
> —John 14:27

26. What do you think would happen if you obeyed the command in 4:6 every time you entered into a disagreement or began to worry? Will you contract with God right now to do this the next time anxiety grips you?

DIGGING DEEPER

When did Paul exemplify healthy peacemaking? Consider, for example, Acts 15 and 21:17–22:29. What other examples can you discover? What do you learn?

27. Paul has exhorted the believers at Philippi to pray in order to overcome anxiety and conflicts. Now he reveals a state of mind that will revolutionize the peacemaking process. What is it (4:8)?

28. What often happens in our minds when we experience conflict? How might meditating on 4:8 facilitate a much healthier peacemaking process?

29. According to Paul, what is yet another way to become a skilled peacemaker (4:9)? Is there someone in your community you can emulate?

30. Specifically, what emotional responses and behavior patterns do you need to change to become a biblical peacemaker in your personal life, working relationships, or ministry life? How do you think Paul would advise you? What consequences might you pay if you refuse to take his admonition seriously?

DIGGING DEEPER

What does God want you to think about when you engage in conflict? What can you learn about God's design for your mind from the following verses: Isaiah 26:3, Luke 10:27, Romans 12:2, and Colossians 3:2?

Make every effort to live in peace with everyone and to be holy; without holiness no one will see the Lord. See to it that no one falls short of the grace of God and that no bitter root grows up to cause trouble and defile many.
—Hebrews 12:14–15

A Contented Generosity | LESSON 8

As a seminary professor I am privileged to hear incredible stories of how God provides for students' needs. Most seminary students live from month to month, trusting that they will scrape together enough to pay their rent, utilities, and transportation, and save enough to pay for next semester's tuition. Life often gets in the way, with an unexpected car repair or doctor's bill. But invariably God intervenes with bags of groceries on the porch or an envelope full of money in the mailbox. I wish you could see the expressions on their faces and the excitement in their voices as they tell me of God's provisions. *Overjoyed* is hardly adequate! I sense God is preparing my students for a lifetime of financial dependence on him through God's people. I expect Paul experienced similar elation when Epaphroditus arrived with a generous gift from the Philippians.

Paul paid his own way, making tents when he could, but his on-the-move lifestyle and packed ministry calendar often hindered him from setting up shop. And when he wrote this letter to the Philippians, he was in prison, completely dependent on others, even for food. The Roman prison system demanded that everyone secure their own meals. The Philippians' gift meant the difference between plenty and hunger.

In this dire setting, Paul rested in the Lord, content and generous. Contentment and generosity are bedfellows, and both require real faith. Pray that God will help us all reach that solid place in our lives so that we can bless others and rest in our own circumstances, whatever they may be, as coming from the hand of a good God.

The old adage "easier said than done" comes to mind, but my earnest prayer is that this lesson will aid in helping us all become contented women with generous spirits. If we think we have this one nailed, a challenge invades our contentment and our fists easily draw tight. Help us, Lord.

Read Philippians 4:10–23.

OPTIONAL

Memorize 1 Timothy 6:6–8

Godliness with contentment is great gain. For we brought nothing into the world, and we can take nothing out of it. But if we have food and clothing, we will be content with that.

How do you measure the quality of your life? What makes it valuable? Perhaps you think in terms of what you have accomplished—your education, your job, your home, your summer house, your clothes, your portfolio, your cars, your art. Jesus said that our lives do not consist of the abundance of possessions. Real life is the life of the mind and the spirit. Real life is freedom from the greed that enslaves us, a freedom that reveals a right relationship with our Maker.
—Vickie Kraft
(*Facing Your Feelings*, 144)

1. Paul continues to praise the Philippians in 4:10. Why are they such a source of delight to him?

2. We learn more about how the Philippians showed their concern for Paul in one of his letters to the Corinthian church. Read 2 Corinthians 8:1–5. What do you learn about the Philippians and their giving history with Paul?

3. What stewardship principles did Paul teach Christians in the following passages?

   2 Corinthians 8:9

   2 Corinthians 9:6–11

   2 Corinthians 9:12–15

DIGGING DEEPER

Using an interlinear Bible resource and an expository dictionary (For example, *The Zondervan Parallel New Testament in Greek and English* and *Vine's Expository Dictionary of New Testament Words*), do a word study on "cheerful" in 2 Corinthians 9:7. What English word comes from this Greek word? How does your word study enlighten your understanding of the verse?

4. What did Paul teach Timothy related to contentment and generosity in 1 Timothy 6:3–10?

5. What great lesson has Paul learned that he wants to pass on to the Philippians and to us (Philippians 4:11)?

6. Paul has experienced various situations in his life. What are the two he cites? What has Paul learned concerning material possessions and physical needs? (4:12–13)

7. Have you learned to be content despite your circumstances? If so, how does this look in your life? If you "know what it is to have plenty" and/or "to be in need," share what you have learned from the experience. How did you learn this valuable lesson?

....

The Secret of Contentment (*12:47 minutes*).

....

8. Specifically, why is Paul so pleased with the Philippians' generosity? What created a special bond between them? (4:14–16)

9. Have you ever experienced a similar bond between yourself and another Christian? Were you on the giving or receiving end? How did this expression of Christian love make you feel?

Put to death, therefore, whatever belongs to your earthly nature: sexual immorality, impurity, lust, evil desires and greed, which is idolatry.
—Colossians 3:5

I can do everything through Christ who gives me strength. With that he transforms his very Stoic-sounding sentence into a sufficiency quite beyond himself, in Christ, the basis and source of everything for Paul. Thus "self-sufficiency" becomes contentment because of his "Christ-sufficiency."
—Gordon Fee (*Philippians*, 186)

Whoever loves money never
   has money enough;
whoever loves wealth is
   never satisfied with their
   income.
This too is meaningless.
As goods increase,
   so do those who consume
   them.
And what benefit are they to
   the owners
   except to feast their eyes on
   them?
The sleep of a laborer is sweet,
   whether they eat little or
   much,
but as for the rich, their
   abundance
   permits them no sleep.
—Ecclesiastes 5:10–12

10. In your opinion, is it more blessed to give or to receive? Why do Christians need to learn to do both graciously?

11. Make a list of the things you believe you need to be content. Analyze your list. Will most of the things on your list bring you lasting joy? Does anything on the list distract you from an intimate walk with Christ?

12. Paul reveals another reason he is pleased that the Philippians have sent him an additional generous gift. What also brings him great joy (4:17–19)?

13. How do contentment and generosity work together? Are these qualities you value and desire?

14. What hinders you from excelling in contentment and generosity? What can you do to overcome these hindrances?

15. Paul signs off by sending greetings from himself, Christians helping him in Rome, and the Roman congregation (4:21–22). Who does he include in verse 22 and what does this inclusion tell you about the gospel's impact in Rome?

16. Compare Paul's benediction (4:23) with his opening words in 1:2. How do you define "grace"? Why is the grace of the Lord Jesus Christ the greatest gift we can possess?

SUMMARY REVIEW QUESTIONS

17. Briefly scan back over the four chapters of Philippians. Can you identify one main theme of the entire book? If so, write out that theme in a phrase or sentence, and explain why you chose this as the main theme.

Sometimes when you get to the end of a novel or short story, there is a moment when something is revealed that makes sense of a mood, a motive, a feeling that has been in the narrative all along. At last we understand why that man was so sad when his dog died. At last we grasp the reason why the old woman had never trusted her sister. Or whatever it is. Philippians ends like that: at last we understand the full extent of why Paul is so grateful for the partnership in the gospel which this church in particular has exercised. It isn't just that they have now sent him money, with Epaphroditus as their willing messenger. It is that this has continued a habit which goes back right to the beginning. This, we see, is why the whole letter has the warm tone, the sense of deep trust and affection, that we have sensed throughout.
—Tom Wright
(*Paul for Everyone*, 135–36)

The Roman Caesar at this time was Nero, and his household included members of the royal family, an army of soldiers, slaves, and freedmen. Archaeologists have excavated the palace and you can visit the site if you travel to Rome today.

The society in the midst of which the Philippian Christians lived might be described as "crooked and depraved," but they were commended for shining there "like stars in the universe" and offering it "the word of life" (2:15–16). Each local church might be compared to a garden planted in a wilderness, but the church's concern was not so much to prevent the wilderness from encroaching on the garden as to see to it that the garden took over more and more of the wilderness. . . . Every church was to be a missionary church, and the history of the expansion of early Christianity shows that many churches realized and fulfilled this mission. Among those that did so the church of Philippi, like the other Macedonian churches, holds an honored place.

—F. F. Bruce (*Philippians*, 162)

18. Listed below are characters mentioned in the letter or people instrumental in the founding of the Philippian church. Briefly, what do you remember about the place and impact of each in your study?

Jesus Christ

Paul

Lydia

The Philippian jailer

The Philippian congregation

Timothy

Epaphroditus

Euodia and Syntyche

19. Which of these people would you like to imitate in your own life and why?

20. Has anyone in your group particularly influenced or encouraged you during this study? If so, make a plan to communicate that to them this week.

21. What do you think you will remember about Paul's letter to the Philippians a year from now? Five years from now? Ten years from now? When you meet Jesus?

22. Congratulations on completing *Philippians: Discovering Joy Through Relationship*. What's next? How do you plan to continue growing closer to Christ through studying God's love letter to you? See www. discovertogetherseries.com for suggestions.

The grace of the Lord Jesus Christ be with your spirit. Amen.

Works Cited

Barash, Susan Shapiro. *Tripping the Prom Queen: The Truth About Women and Rivalry*. New York: St. Martin's Press, 2006.

Bentley, Michael. *Shining in the Darkness: Philippians Simply Explained*. Grange Close, England: Evangelical Press, 1997.

Bruce, F. F. *Philippians*. Understanding the Bible Commentary Series. Grand Rapids: Baker Books, 1989.

Companjen, Anneke. *Singing Through the Night: Courageous Stories of Faith from Women in the Persecuted Church*. Grand Rapids: Revell, 2007.

Constable, Thomas L. *Notes on Acts*. 2015 edition. www.soniclight.com /constable/notes/pdf/acts.pdf. Used by permission.

Dawn, Marva. *Truly the Community*. Grand Rapids: Eerdmans, 1992.

Fee, Gordon. *Philippians*. The IVP New Testament Commentary Series. Downers Grove, IL: IVP Academic, 1999.

Gangel, Kenneth, and Samuel Canine. *Communication and Conflict Management in Churches and Christian Organizations*. Eugene, OR: Wipf and Stock, 2002.

Gorman, Julie. *Community That Is Christian*. Grand Rapids: Baker Books, 2002.

Heim, Pat, and Susan Murphy. *In the Company of Women*. New York: Jeremy P. Tarcher/Putnam, 2003.

Kraft, Vickie. *Facing Your Feelings*. Dallas, TX: Word Publishing, 1996.

Longenecker, Richard N. "Acts," *John–Acts*. Vol. 9. The Expositor's Bible Commentary. Edited by Frank E. Gaebelein and J. D. Douglas. Grand Rapids: Zondervan, 1981.

Maxwell, John. *Winning with People: Discover the People Principles That Work for You Every Time*. Nashville, TN: Thomas Nelson, 2004.

Ogilve, Lloyd John. *Drumbeat of Love: The Unlimited Power of the Spirit as Revealed in the Book of Acts*. Waco, TX: Word Books, 1980.

Packer, J. I. *Knowing God*. Downer's Grove, IL: InterVarsity Press, 1973.

Shirer, Priscilla Evans. *He Speaks to Me: Preparing to Hear From God*. Chicago, IL: Moody Publishers, 2006.

Stone, Douglas, Bruce Patton, and Sheila Heen. *Difficult Conversations*. New York: Penguin Books, 1999.

Strauss, Richard L. *The Joy of Knowing God*. Neptune, NJ: Loizeaux Brothers, 1984.

Swindoll, Charles R. *Laugh Again: Experience Outrageous Joy*. Dallas, TX: Word Publishing, 1992.

———. *Tale of the Tardy Oxcart: And 1,501 Other Stories*. Nashville, TN: Word Publishing, 1998.

Walvoord, John F. *Jesus Christ Our Lord*. Chicago, IL: Moody Publishers, 1969.

White, John. *Daring to Draw Near*. Downers Grove, IL: InterVarsity Press, 1977.

Winebrenner, Jan. *Intimate Faith: A Woman's Guide to the Spiritual Disciplines*. New York: Warner Books, 2003.

Winner, Lauren. *Mudhouse Sabbath: An Invitation to a Life of Spiritual Discipline*. Brewster, MA: Paraclete Press, 2007.

Wright, Tom. *Paul for Everyone: The Prison Letters*. Louisville, KY: Westminster John Knox Press, 2003.

Yancey, Philip. *What's So Amazing About Grace?* Grand Rapids: Zondervan, 1997.

About the Author

Sue Edwards is associate professor of educational ministries and leadership (her specialization is women's studies) at Dallas Theological Seminary, where she has the opportunity to equip men and women for future ministry. She brings over thirty years of experience into the classroom as a Bible teacher, curriculum writer, and overseer of several megachurch women's ministries. As minister to women at Irving Bible Church and director of women's ministry at Prestonwood Baptist Church in Dallas, she has worked with women from all walks of life, ages, and stages. Her passion is to see modern and postmodern women connect, learn from one another, and bond around God's Word. Her Bible studies have ushered thousands of women all over the country and overseas into deeper Scripture study and community experiences.

With Kelley Mathews, Sue has coauthored *New Doors in Ministry to Women: A Fresh Model for Transforming Your Church, Campus, or Mission Field*; *Women's Retreats: A Creative Planning Guide*; and *Leading Women Who Wound: Strategies for an Effective Ministry*. Sue and Kelley joined with Henry Rogers to coauthor *Mixed Ministry: Working Together as Brothers and Sisters in an Oversexed Society*. Her newest book, coauthored with Barbara Neumann, *Organic Mentoring: A Mentor's Guide to Relationships with Next Generation Women*, explores the new values, preferences, and problems of the next generation and shows mentors how to avoid potential land mines and how to mentor successfully.

Sue has a doctor of ministry degree from Gordon-Conwell Theological Seminary in Boston and a master's in Bible from Dallas Theological Seminary. With Dr. Joye Baker, she oversees the Dallas Theological Seminary doctor of ministry degree in Christian education with a women-in-ministry emphasis.

Sue has been married to David for over forty years. They have two married daughters, Heather and Rachel, and five grandchildren. David is a retired CAD applications engineer, a lay prison chaplain, and founder of their church's prison ministry.